The Guardianship of the Jurist and the Theory of Islamic Governance

A Historical Perspective

ʿAllamah Sayyid Jaʿfar Murtaḍā al-ʿĀmilī

AL-BURĀQ

Copyright

ISBN: 978-1-956276-26-8
Printed and published by al-Burāq Publications.
Translated and annotated by al-Burāq Publications. Where needed, context and transliterations were added. Some minor edits were made to the translated Arabic text.

www.al-Buraq.org
publications@al-Buraq.org

First Edition | September 2022

Dedication

The publication of this book was made possible through the generous support of our donors.

Please recite *Sūrat al-Fātiha* and ask God for the Divine reward (*thawāb*) to be conferred upon the donors and also the souls of all the deceased in whose memory their loved ones have contributed graciously towards the publication of *The Guardianship of the Jurist and the Theory of Islamic Governance: A Historical Perspective.*

We begin by giving all praise and thanks to God ﷻ for giving us the tawfiq to translate this book. He has guided us and without Him, we would not have been guided to the straight path embodied by the Prophet Muḥammad ﷺ and the Ahl al-Bayt عليهم السلام.

This book is dedicated to all the scholars, martyrs and believers who worked tirelessly to promote the pure Muḥammadan path.

We want to also give our thanks and appreciation to all believers from around the world and acknowledge the team which helped al-Burāq Publications complete this work, spending countless hours to make its publication possible. Please recite Sūrat al-Fātiḥah on behalf of them, their families, and their marḥūmīn.

This book is dedicated in honor of the following individuals. Please remember them in your prayers and may God ﷻ have mercy on them and their loved ones.

Ali Ftouni

Ali Shahine

Alya Agemy

Bande Khuda

Basheerunnisa Begum

Dalal Hourani

Fatima Mohessin

Ghalie Hourani

Habiba Sakha

Hajj Ahmad Youssef

Hajj Hassan Sobh

Hajj Ismail Y. Abadi

Hajj Moussa A. Hamzi

Hajj Sami Ftouni

Hajj Youssef Najdi

Hajji Amneh Sobh-Ftouni

Hajji Hiam Hojeije

Hajji Shahina Saad

Hajji Zahiyah Kasir

Humayun Ali Baig

Imane Srour

Inaam Jaffal

Kadhum Shakarchi

Kobra Rustami

Lyal Nichols

Nurul H. Jafri

Sabiha Jafri

Samira Alizada

Sayyid Khaled M. Saleh

Sayyid Sobh H. Sobh

Shahīd Ibrahim Hadi

Shahīd Mohammad H. Tholfagari

Shahīd Mohsen Hojaji

Sydney Johnson

Turfah Sobh

William Troupe Sr.

Zaara Ali

Duʿāʾ al-Ḥujjah

اللَّهُمَّ كُنْ لِوَلِيِّكَ الْحُجَّةِ بْنِ الْحَسَنِ صَلَوَاتُكَ

عَلَيْهِ وَعَلَى آبَائِهِ فِي هَذِهِ السَّاعَةِ وَفِي كُلِّ

سَاعَةٍ وَلِيّاً وَحَافِظاً وَقَائِداً وَنَاصِراً وَدَلِيلاً

وَعَيْناً حَتَّى تُسْكِنَهُ أَرْضَكَ طَوْعاً وَتُمَتِّعَهُ فِيهَا طَوِيلاً

O God, be, for Your representative, the Ḥujjat (proof), son of al-Ḥasan, Your blessings be upon him and his forefathers, in this hour and in every hour: a guardian, a protector, a leader, a helper, a proof, and an eye - until You make him live on the Earth, in obedience (to You), and cause him to live in it for a long time.

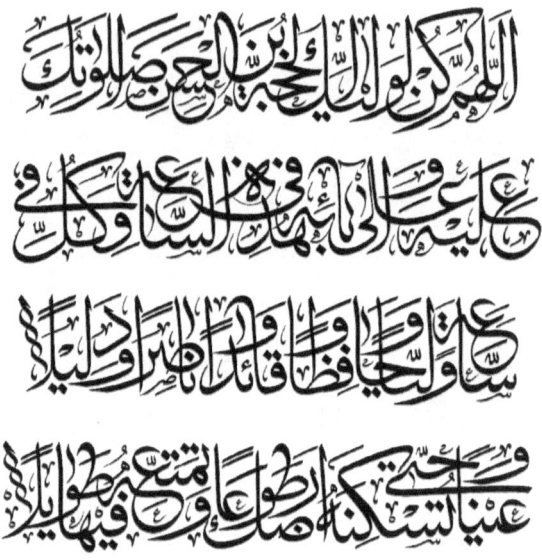

Terms of Respect

The following Arabic phrases have been used throughout this book in their respective places to show the reverence which the noble personalities deserve.

عزّ وجلّ

Used for God, meaning:
Exalted and Sublime (Perfect) is He

صلى الله عليه وآله

Used for Prophet Muḥammad, meaning:
Blessings from God be upon him and his family

عليه السلام

Used for a man (singular) of a high status, meaning:
Peace be upon him

عليها السلام

Used for a woman (singular) of a high status, meaning:
Peace be upon her

عليهما السلام

Used for men/women (dual) of a high status, meaning:
Peace be upon them both

عليهم السلام

Used for men and/or women (plural) of a high status, meaning:
Peace be upon them all

عجل الله تعالى فرجه الشريف

Used for Imām Muḥammad al-Mahdī, meaning:
May God hasten his return

قدس سره

Used for a deceased scholar, meaning:
May his resting [burial] place remain pure

Transliteration Table

The method of transliteration of Islamic terminology from the Arabic language has been carried out according to the standard transliteration table below.

ء	ʾ	ر	r	ف	f
ا	a	ز	z	ق	q
ب	b	س	s	ك	k
ت	t	ش	sh	ل	l
ث	th	ص	ṣ	م	m
ج	j	ض	ḍ	ن	n
ح	ḥ	ط	ṭ	و	w
خ	kh	ظ	ẓ	ه	h
د	d	ع	ʿ	ي	y
ذ	dh	غ	gh		
Long Vowels					
ا	ā	و	ū	ي	ī
Short Vowels					
ـَـ	a	ـُـ	u	ـِـ	i

Table of Contents

About the Author

Sayyid Ja'far Murtaḍā al-'Āmilī, son of the late Sayyid Muṣṭafā Murtaḍā al-'Āmilī, was born on the 25th of Ṣafar, 1364 (January 6, 1945), in a southern Lebanese town called *Dayr Qānūn Rās al-'Ain*, where his father had lived for several years, and then returned to his hometown, *'Aithā al-Zuṭ*, which was later changed to the name *'Aithā al-Jabal*, *Bint Jbayl* district, where he settled.

He began religious studies at a young age at the hand of his father, and then went to Najaf, 'Irāq to pursue his scientific education in 1382 AH (1962 AD).

In Ḥawzah, he studied the introductory and most of the intermediate subjects, and in the year 1388 AH (1968 AD) he decided to move to the religious seminary in the *Holy City of Qum*, upon the request of his father (may God have mercy on him) and the approval of an *Istikhārat*.

Sayyid Ja'far had specialized writings in the field of history and was distinctive in terms of investigation and examination. He participated in *al-Ḥadd* in the field of research and storytelling in order to preserve the 'Alawīte

Muḥammadan heritage and purify it from impurities.

He recited poetry at a young age, with his father telling him "I want you to be a scholar, not a poet," and then showed him examples of leading scholars who were known for their poetry and forgotten for their religious specificity.

In the *Holy City of Qum*, he established religious schools, in addition to other various programs.

Sayyid Jaʿfar participated in many scientific conferences in Irān and other countries and contributed to the establishment of the "Arabic School" that is affiliated with the Ḥawzah in the Holy City of Qum.

After 25 years of residence in *Qum*, he returned to *Jabal ʿĀmīl* [modern day South Lebanon] in 1414 (1993) and remained in Lebanon for the rest of his life.

Sayyid Jaʿfar established a religious school in Lebanon and named it "the Ḥawzah of Imām ʿAlī ibn Abī Ṭālib ﷺ. In addition, he also established the Islamic Center for Studies.

Sayyid Jaʿfar taught advanced ḥawzah lessons in Bayrūt and he followed his weekly lessons with the interpretation of the Noble Qurʾān and Islamic and religious culture.

Sayyid Jaʿfar is the author of over 200 books, including biographies of the Holy Prophet ﷺ (35 volumes), Imām ʿAlī ﵇ (53 volumes) and Imām al-Ḥusayn ﵇ (24 volumes). Even after being diagnosed and treated for cancer, he continued to write.

On Ṣafar 27, 1441 (October 26, 2019) Sayyid Jaʿfar Murtaḍā passed away in a hospital in Bayrūt and was buried in his hometown of *ʿAithā al-Jabal.*

In short, Sayyid Jaʿfar spent his lifetime in servitude of the religion of Islam. If we were to sum his lifelong work and effort into words, we would not be able to do him justice. He was a historian, a prolific author, and a jurist who defended the truth and preserved the history of Islam. We ask God ﷻ to grant him a lofty rank with the Ahl al-Bayt ﵈ and reward him for his unwavering devotion.

Preface

بسم الله الرحمن الرحيم

In the Name of God, the Beneficent, the Merciful

Praise be to God, the Lord of all the Worlds, and peace and benediction be upon the best of His creations and the pure immaculate members of his Household and may God's curse be on their enemies, from this moment until the day of Judgment.

I have previously written about the topic of "the guardianship of the jurist in the Ṣaḥīḥa of 'Umar b. Ḥanẓala" where I tackled – in the introduction – the subject of the guardianship of the jurist and its rational and primordial proofs. Nonetheless, what was written there was not comprehensive of all the aspects of that study, for, it aimed at presenting the issue from a specific angle which aligns with the nature of an introduction to the topic. Here, I wanted to raise the issue from a different aspect, whilst emphasizing on the necessity of reading what was written before – for both writings are complementary – and pointing out the fact that some other aspects are still in need of further study and investigation. Perhaps, we may be successful in having another opportunity for that if so God wills.

18, Jamāda al-Awwal, 1404 AH

February 1984

Qum

Sayyid Ja'far Murtaḍā al-'Āmilī

Introduction

God ﷻ said in the Noble Qur'ān:

﴾Your guardian is only God, His Apostle, and the faithful who maintain the prayer and give the zakāt while bowing down.﴿[1]

This noble verse tackled the guardianship of God ﷻ and His Messenger ﷺ, in addition to a few believers who possess certain traits and who – after him – attain the guardianship and government over the people.

We do not want to study this verse from a historical, political, theological, narrative or interpretational perspective. Rather, we want to know the position of this verse - from an Islamic viewpoint – in terms of a governmental system which dominates all the affairs, behaviors and movements of the nation, in addition to directing its stances in regards to its life and journey towards its goal. Islam takes care to guide the nation towards this goal, and then realize and acquire it.

We are not interested in tackling the various theories and theses on the definition and form of the governmental system, which were

---

[1] Sūrat al-Mā'idah, Verse 55.

thoroughly discussed by scholars and intellectuals, or accepted by people themselves during a period of time or another, or imposed by specific circumstances that were endured by nations in different eras. Such as the democratic system, which they claim to be the so-called government of the people and the workers. Or the government of the most powerful dictatorship, amongst others that were used from time to time as a slogan that aims to attract people and drag them behind those ambitious and exploiting individuals, or ones that were actually adopted by the people without any hidden agenda behind it.

Perhaps we may find some who claim that there is no need for a government at all.

However, we do not want to delve into any of these matters nor its likes through research, criticism and investigation. We only want to make an attempt to know Islam's opinion in regards to government and the governor, and to see whether it meets any of the proposed theories or others that were known across the nations, or has a new and unique proposal in this field.

Government is a Necessity that Arises from the Primordial Nature

In order to start approaching the main topic of this study, we must point out the following:

Islam believes in the necessity of having a dominant governor who works on imposing order and preventing chaos. By adopting this opinion, Islam aligns with reality and with the primordial nature which can neither be denied nor debated.

Imām ʿAlī ﷺ said, "The Imāmate is the governmental order of the nation."[2]

He ﷺ also said, "There must be a government, and sustenance for the governor...etc."[3]

He ﷺ also said, "People must have a leader, virtuous or licentious, under whose command

[2] al-Tamīmī, ʿAbd al-Wāḥid, *Ghurar al-Hikam wa Durar al-Kalim* Vol. 1, p. 36. and (in the same work) Vol. 2, p. 525, *al-"Amāna w al-Amānat"*. Also referenced from Sharīf Raḍī, Muḥammad b. al-Ḥusayn, *Nahj al-Balāgha*, Sermon/Letter/Saying 252.

[3] al-Nuʿmān, al-Qāḍī, *Daʿāʾim al-Islam*, Vol. 2, p. 538.

the believer works and the disbeliever enjoys himself. Through him, God delivers the terms, collects the spoils and fights the enemy. Through him, paths become secure and the weak are given (justice) against the powerful, until the virtuous find peace and people get relieved from the licentious."[4]

[4] Sharīf Raḍī, Muḥammad b. al-Ḥusayn, *Nahj al-Balāgha* (with commentary by Abdo), Sermon/Letter/Saying 39.
Also review:

a. al-Muttaqī al-Hindī, ʾAlī, *Kanz al-ʿummāl fī sunan al-aqwāl wa l-afʿāl*, Vol. 11, p. 309 and 286, and Vol. 5, p. 448.
b. al-Yaʿqūbī, ʾAḥmad, *Tārīkh al-Yaʿqūbī*, Vol. 2, p. 209.
c. al-Balādhurī, Aḥmad, *Ansāb al-Ashrāf* (researched by al-Maḥmoudī) Vol. 2, p. 352 and p. 377.
d. Majlisī, ʿAllāma Muḥammad Bāqir, *Biḥār al-Anwār*, Vol. 75, p. 352.

It was also implied by: Q Wahab, ʿAbdul Razzāq, Ibn Jarir, and Khashīsh, in *al-Istīqama*, and it was transferred to the sources of *Nahj al-Balāgha* Vol. 1, p. 440 from *Qūt al-Qulūb* Vol. 1, p. 530 and others.

He ﷺ also said, "A vicious lion is better than an oppressive ruler, and an oppressive ruler is better than incessant dilemmas."[5]

Imām ʿAlī al-Riḍā ﷺ said, as he was mentioning the reasons for having the rulers and affairs compliant with the Imāms, "And among them: is that we do not find any denomination or creed sustaining without set values and leadership critical for their religious affairs. For, it is not possible for the Wise Creator to leave the people without that which He knows is necessary and indispensable for them; for, through him, they fight their enemy, divide their spoils, establish their gatherings and collectiveness and protect their oppressed from their oppressors."[6]

---

[5] Majlisī, ʿAllamah Muḥammad Bāqir, *Biḥār al-Anwār*, Vol. 75, p. 359. Review: *Dustūr Maʿālim al-Hikam* p. 170, *Ghurar al-Hikam wa Durar al-Kalim* Vol. 1, p. 437 and Vol. 2, p. 784.

[6] Ṣadūq, Shaykh Muḥammad b. ʿAlī, *ʿUyūn ʾAkhbār ar-Riḍā*, Vol. 2, p. 101, Ṣadūq, Shaykh Muḥammad b. ʿAlī, *ʿIlal al-Sharāyiʿ*, Vol. 1, p. 253, and al-ʿArūsī al-Ḥuwayzī, *Tafsīr Nūr al-Thaqalayn*, Vol. 1, p. 412-413. Review: al-Ansārī, Shaykh Murtaḍā b. Muḥammad, *al-Makāsib*, p. 153.

In these words, they ﷺ are informing us about the law of primordial nature, nature and reality which stipulates the necessity of a ruler. Herein, they are not tackling the issue from a legislative viewpoint; for, the government of a licentious person is impermissible and utterly rejected under Islam. For, the words of Imām ʿAlī b. Abī Ṭālib and Imām ʿAlī al-Riḍā ﷺ which prefer the vicious lion over the oppressive ruler indicate this matter clearly.

Based on the above, there is no room left to listen to those who say: there is no need for a ruler, and there is no need for a system. For, this saying does not rely on any justification – not on a theoretical level nor on the external realistic level.

This is in regard to the ruling of Islam and the primordial nature which necessitate the existence of a ruler.

Introduction to the Study

Based on the above, we say: The Islamic perception towards the political system which is supposed to control the movement of the nation towards its aspired goal is completely aligned with the primordial nature as well. For, it is not distant from man's perception, imaginings or ambitions. That is why it is necessary for anyone who wants to learn about the Islamic opinion in this regard to refer back to the primordial nature.

Before going further into our objectives, we want to point out that we must - first and foremost- remember the following:

1. First, one must exert efforts in the attempt of knowing that noble goal towards which Islam guides the nation, and which it works for the sake of realizing and attaining.

2. It is crucial to get acquainted with the Islamic viewpoint towards existence and life, and to know whether it perceives the worldly life as the ultimate thing, or it believes that this worldly life has an everlasting extension, perpetuation and future continuity which surpasses this life

towards a more expansive, perfect and complete horizon.

3. The nature of the system that is supposed to govern the nation's journey, movements and stances is determined based on the nature of that goal, and in accordance with the viewpoint towards existence and life.

In regards to the first point: We do not hesitate to emphasize on the fact that the goal is to lead the human being, as an individual and a nation, towards absolute, holistic and real well-being. This happiness does not end with the termination of his life in this world; it rather persists through the ages to become perpetual, everlasting, and eternal.

As for the second point: Islam considers the worldly life to be a preparatory stage preceding the eternal life such that man is transferred from this stage onto another wider and more expansive stage where man's humanity is materialized and where he gets to experience his true self in a lively, realistic and deep manner. This has been emphasized by many verses and absolute religious texts; moreover, it is one of Islam's primary axioms whereby it does not require any proof or testament.

Accordingly, the third point becomes clearer from the Islamic viewpoint; for, it considers that the system which is supposed to govern man's life and his entire relationships must lead man towards that noble goal; as it must observe – while designing its legislations – connecting man to God ﷻ, so he can constantly live in the shades of Divine Care and benefit – as much as possible – from the Divine Teachings which are manifested in absolute obedience and sincere worship of God ﷻ.

﴾I did not create the jinn and the humans except that they may worship Me.﴿[7]

Therefore, it is only natural that the Islamic theory of political government is aligned with its viewpoint towards existence, life and man, and that it assesses man's relationship with the worldly life and his surroundings correctly and give it its proper place and role that it is

---

[7] Sūrat al-Dhāriyāt, Verse 56.

supposed to play throughout man's journey in the eternal life towards his noble goal. Man gets attracted towards this goal by being connected, in all his stances and deeds, to God ﷻ and through pure proximity from Him ﷻ.

Necessary Elements

In pursuit of achieving the above, it is natural that such government – nay any government – requires the following elements:

1. Being aware and comprehensive of all that may guarantee the realization of that goal or support in reaching it.

   This includes: Knowledge of everything that surrounds the life of the community to be governed – be it small or large – such as circumstances and conditions that have direct or indirect impact on his perfection and movement.

2. To be safe from error in understanding the reality of the circumstances and conditions, and capable of distinguishing the reforming agent from the corrupting one. The same applies to the practical and executive field. He (the ruler) must also possess absolute immunity which enables him to prevent any form of injustice, oppression or exploitation, starting from personal belongings and other things which do not benefit those whose affairs and interests he is supposed to be managing and overseeing.

3. To have the motive that guarantees a powerful and continuous movement in the right direction and the readiness to endure the hardships and troubles that may arise due to the nature of the mission which he is supposed to carry out responsibly and be well acquainted with.

   This is in addition to the general conditions that must be met – at least in its minimum standards – in a leader's personality, even in regards to a small community with few supplies and a small number of citizens, such as: intellect, bravery, power and others.

Natural Basics

If we observe a human being8 once he is born, we see that he lives through the phase of childhood where he is incapable of fulfilling his needs by himself or making the most beneficial choice. We will realize that he is submissive to the rule and power of his parents who manage and oversee his affairs and direct all his movements and idleness towards that which they claim is in his best interest and more appropriate to his current life and future, as they are the most knowledgeable of his conditions and surrounding circumstances.

In fact, the happiest family and that which is most distant from trouble and turmoil is the family that is governed, ruled and – whose affairs are – supervised by one person who is naturally the father, since he is the most powerful and competent to secure its needs - especially the needs of the weakest individual thereof. Furthermore, he is the most capable of protecting him from any external violation to which he may be exposed or from natural changes which may carry within it a sort of harshness, even in normal situations, towards this vulnerable being.

---

[8] Or every newborn, even an animal.

Moreover, when a father carries out his government over the small community, he acts – in his stances, rulings and procedures – from the spirit of compassion, tenderness and ensuring the general interest, as much as possible. He impulsively and naturally takes care of the preservation of the growing existence of the family in a way that allows it to move towards the path of perfection and realize its desired goals in the future.

In other words, if we suppose there is a family composed of a father, mother and children, it will naturally aim at achieving a certain goal in this life, be it comfort, peacefulness, tranquility and happiness, building the universe, all of these or elsewise.

This goal requires a movement that is directed towards it in pursuit of realizing this goal. And this movement cannot be random; for, random movements do not lead towards a goal except within a probability of one in a million. And rational people do not build their lives upon such reasoning.

Therefore, there must be a system that governs, organizes and directs this movement, balances between the desires, movements and silences of this and that person, and preserves them from conflicting with others' movements and stances and other universal beings which surround them, even if this system was established by human intellect, wisdom and planning.

In any case, this requires the presence of someone who oversees this movement and its submissiveness to that system which must control the journey and act as the arbitrator who makes decisions in regards to its affairs and problems and as the system which supports it in overcoming the obstacles encountered and protects it from natural or unnatural dilemmas.

The father is the most fitting and competent person to shoulder this mission; for, he possesses the capacity which allows him to do so on one hand, and the wisdom, rationality and balance, in addition to a sufficient extent of emotion which manages to maintain the best interest of this family. Moreover, it represents a guarantee from falling into injustice and aggression, leniency and extremism, or indifference towards its affairs and problems.

Based on the above, it becomes clear that the father usually possesses an acceptable figure of the elements which we have mentioned previously, that effectively help him in carrying out the affairs of that small community which fall under his control. And if he loses some of these elements, then the religious ruler – and even rational people – will suspend his right to government and control over that family.

Whereas when the father has many children, and then grandchildren, then his capacity for managing affairs and comprehending much of the circumstances and situations that have positive or negative implications within the scope of his reign which fall under his government - this capacity – will weaken in comparison to a small family. Moreover, the compassion which represents the power of motion and movement will weaken as the descendants increase and as the kinship medians diversify and multiply. This leads to the feebleness of the connection which attracts them to him, and him to them, or at least to some of them whenever he finds in others what satisfies him emotionally and psychologically, or whenever he finds in some of them resistance or disobedience which distances him from taking care of their affairs and causes him to prioritize the interests of others over theirs – which happens a lot of times. Accordingly, his personal tendencies will dominate a lot of his stances and he will face a lot of issues with weakness, feebleness and indifference when his interests favor his own comfort over the interest of all or some of those who are under his government and care – as we witness in the western communities today. And there are not any other guarantees that prevent this from happening or mitigate its risks and impact. We have seen some parents who – whenever their child commits a wrongdoing – do not stop at hitting him to discipline him, but rather exceed that towards taking revenge from him in many situations.

However, when a family expands to become a tribe, and the tribe grows to become a village, then this weakness will grow respectively and become more effective in causing weakness and instability in the social foundations of the area which lies under his reign. Corruption, which will follow the hardships and pains, will find the convenient opportunity to leak towards the life of that community and negatively impact the reality of those people and then their future.

As for the case where his domination and reign covers a district or a state, then this weakness and that corruption will become clearer and its impact will become deeper and more widespread, although the scope of the area under his reign demands – nay necessitates – the increase in his motive force and personal capacities to confront the large needs and plenty problems which may encounter them. The scope also emphasizes the necessity of deepening and embedding the psychological faculties which represent greater immunity from falling into error or from inflicting injustice upon others or the dominion of his psychological tendencies and others over him. This is in addition to the certain need for further knowledge and comprehension of the circumstances and conditions of those who fall within the scope of his work and area of coverage.

The Primordial Nature of the Government of the Prophets and Guardians

If we look at the government of the Prophets and Guardians 🕮, who shoulder the mission of leading the movement of mankind entirely, we will realize that it does not part from these precepts established by the primordial nature and the natural path. However, the mission of the Prophets 🕮 is greater, since it affects the lives of entire nations and lives of generations that are yet to come. Accordingly, the requirement of possessing these elements must be met by them in a more perfect manner, especially if their message is universal and they aim at confronting the diverse nations with righteousness, guiding them and taking care of them by carrying out the thorough process of destruction and rebuilding of the social, psychological, intellectual, political, and economic and other foundations.

For this purpose, we find that the Prophets and their Guardians 🕮, especially our great Prophet Muḥammad 🕮 and the Imāms from his progeny ﷺ[9], have realized the level of immaculateness in regards to guaranteeing the fact that their actions are aligned with wisdom which is supposed to dominate all relationships and connections, in addition to guaranteeing their abstention from falling into error, injustice, aggressions or recklessness in carrying out their mission – which is something that a father may sometimes fall in. For, any mistake, aggression or recklessness – no matter how small – will have an expansive and thorough impact which will affect the entire world and spread to the extent that influences people's lives, nation after nation, and generation after the other, until God ﷻ wishes.

If the father has a comprehensive understanding of the objective circumstances surrounding the family, we find that the prophets possess a complete and holistic awareness and knowledge of what reforms and what corrupts; for, they are

[9] There is only one difference, which is that the Prophets ﷺ receive their knowledge through revelation, and thereby connect to God ﷻ. Whereas, the Imāms ﷺ receive their knowledge through the Prophets ﷺ.

connected to the immaterial world and receive
divine revelation in this regard.

With respect to other personal capacities, they
possess great competencies and unique
characteristics that are sufficient to make them
capable of understanding all the circumstances
and conditions, and enduring the burdens of
the leadership which guides towards the path of
anticipated happiness.

And so, in regards to the motive force and its
continuity, this Prophet and Imām 🕮 possess a
great deal of love and compassion towards the
nation – the entire nation – even towards those
who fight them and aim at destroying them and
their movement. In fact, the Prophet 🕮 would
feel great agony and empathy towards them.
The history of the Prophets and Imāms 🕮, in
addition to all the difficulties and dilemmas they
have endured for the sake of guiding their
nation and leading them out of the darkness
towards the light, is the best testament to what
we are saying. Moreover, the Noble Qur'ān has
narrated to us the hardships encountered by
Nūḥ, Ibrāhīm, Mūsā, ʿĪsā, Lūṭ, and other

Prophets ﷺ with their nations and people. As for our Prophet Muḥammad ﷺ, he faced an abundance of difficulties and dilemmas which exceeded those encountered by any of the prophets who preceded him, to the extent that it was narrated the he ﷺ said, "No one was harmed as much as I was."[10]

Our Noble Prophet ﷺ has reached, through his tenderness, compassion and love towards the nation, in addition to his sincere sacrifice for its sake, the ultimate goal; and he fulfilled his vow completely. God ﷻ highlighted this feature, which is actually one of his qualifications as a leader and not as an individual. He ﷻ said:

﴾*There has certainly come to you an apostle from among yourselves. Grievous to him is your distress; he has deep concern for you, and is most kind and merciful to the faithful.*﴿[11]

---

[10] al-Manāwi, *Kunūz al-Ḥaqā'iq* (in the footnotes of al-Suyūṭī, 'Abd al-Raḥmān b. Abī Bakr, *al-Jāmi' al-Saghīr*), Vol. 2, p. 82-83, and Vol. 2, p. 144.

[11] Sūrat al-Tawbah, Verse 128.

He ﷻ also said:

﴾*You are liable to imperil*[12] *your life for their sake, if they should not believe this discourse, out of grief.*﴿[13]

And He ﷻ says:

﴾*So do not fret yourself to death regretting for them.*﴿[14]

There are other verses as well that portray the Prophet's ﷺ care for guiding his people, which cannot be measured.[15]

As for Imām 'Alī ؑ, his heart was filled with pain even though, in his eyes, their caliphate was not worth an old shoe horn. He only cared about establishing righteousness or annul

---

[12] Torment (*al-bukhou'*): exerting great efforts, and Bakha' Nafsahu (torment himself) means to kill oneself out of affection or anger (Shartūnī, Sa'īd al-Khūrī, *Aqrab al-Mawārid fī Faṣḥ al-'Arabīyah wa-al-Shawārid*, Vol. 1, p. 32).

[13] Sūrat al-Kahf, Verse 6.

[14] Sūrat Fāṭir, Verse 8.

[15] Sūrat al-Naḥl, Verse 37, and Sūrat Yūsuf, Verse 103.

falsehood. To him, their worldly life was more worthless than a sheep's sneeze, as per his declarations.

In fact, he only endured the difficult struggles and heavy troubles imposed by the people for the sake of the people. For, He ﷺ is with them as the poet says:

"I want his life and he wants my death, who would excuse me and blame my Muradi friend?"

ʿAlī and I are the Fathers of this Nation

Based on the aforementioned, we deeply understand what the Prophet ﷺ aims for by saying the following to Imām ʿAlī ؑ, "ʿAlī and I are the fathers of this nation."[16]

For, he is the one who manages and controls from the basis of wisdom which dominates his stances, and affection which leads him to sacrifice for their sake and endure all sorts of trouble, struggle, pain and trials for them.

We also realize the purpose of the numerous divine orders in the Noble Qurʾān and on the tongues of the Prophet ﷺ and Imāms ؑ between these two fathers and their love. For, it

---

[16] Review:

a. al-Baḥrānī, Hāshim al-Tūbilī, *Tafsīr al-Burhān*, Vol. 1, p. 369 (commentary by Ibn Shahrāshūb)
b. al-Zamakhsharī, *al-Fāʾiq fī Gharīb al-Ḥadīth*
c. Majlisī, ʿAllāma Muḥammad Bāqir, *Biḥār al-Anwār*, Vol. 16, p. 95, and Vol. 40 p. 45
d. Ṣadūq, Shaykh Muḥammad b. ʿAlī, *Maʿānī al-Akhbār* p. 52; *ʿUyūn Akhbār al-Riḍā*, Vol. 2 p. 85; *Ilal al-Sharāyiʿ* p. 127.
e. Ṭabāṭabāʾī, ʿAllāma Sayyid Muḥammad Ḥusayn, *al-Mīzān fī Tafsīr al-Qurʾān*, Vol. 4, p. 357

is narrated that Imām Ja'far al-Sādiq ﷺ said about God's ﷻ saying:

﴾*We have enjoined man to be good to his parents.*﴿[17]

He said, "The Messenger of God ﷺ is one of the fathers."

Muḥammad b. 'Ijlān said, "And who is the other?"

He said, 'Alī."[18]

The Prophet ﷺ said, "The right of 'Alī b. Abī Ṭālib upon this nation (and in other narrations

[17] Sūrat al-'Ankabūt, Verse 8.

[18] al-'Asqalānī, Ḥafīẓ b. Ḥajar, *Lisān al-Mīzān*, Vol. 2, p. 40.

"upon every Muslim") is like the right of the father upon his son."[19]

In this context, uncountable narrations were mentioned which do not fit this study and ought to be reviewed in its proper place.[20]

Therefore, we point out the fact that the pain, catastrophes and trials endured by the Prophets and Guardians ﷺ in the path of their

---

[19] As found in:

a. adh-Dhahabī, Shams ad-Dīn, *Mizān al-I'tidāl*, Vol. 3, p. 316.
b. al-'Asqalānī, Ḥafīẓ b. Ḥajar, *Lisān al-Mizān*, Vol. 4, p. 399.
c. al-Juwaynī, Ibrāhīm, *Farā'id al-Simatayn,* Vol. 1, p. 397.
d. al-Khawārazmī, *al-Manāqib,* p. 219 and 230.
e. al-Ṭūsī, Shaykh Muḥammad b. al-Ḥasan, *al-Amālī*, Vol. 2, p. 277.
f. Ibn al-Maghāzlī, *Manāqīb al-Imām 'Alī b. Abī Tālib* ؑ, p. 48.
g. The Imām 'Alī ؑ translation for Ibn 'Askar (verified by al-Maḥmoudī) Vol. 2, p. 271-272 which was transferred by al-Maḥmūdī from *Ghāyat al-Marām*, p. 544.

[20] Review: al-Baḥrānī, Hāshim al-Tūbilī, *Tafsīr al-Burhān*, Vol. 3, p. 244-245, 294, and Majlisī, 'Allāma Muḥammad Bāqir, *Biḥār al-Anwār*, Vol. 75, p. 356.

summoning towards God ﷻ is in fact one of the harshest things that can be confronted by man in his emotional life. Nay it is more severe than the stroke of a sword and the approach of death. For, one of the harshest and most difficult things shouldered by man is to melt in love and care, sacrifice all that is precious and valuable, endure all that is abhorrent and suffer through pains for the sake of the life and happiness of a person, and then to find out that this person, in particular, is immersed in grudges towards him and sacrifices everything he has to get rid of him, hurt him and even kill him and nip him – and everyone close to him - in the bud. This person accepts his way only for the sake of granting him life and happiness and protecting him from every trial and struggle. Yes, this is the true meaning of sincerity and love; whereby there is not any trace of a personal interest, or a material or moral benefit which befalls this person.

'Alī and I are the Fathers of this Nation

And God ﷻ pointed out this by saying:

﴾Say, *'Do not count it as a favor to me your embracing of Islam. Rather it is God who has done you a favor in that He has guided you to faith, should you be truthful.*﴿[21]

[21] Sūrat al-Ḥujurāt, Verse 17.

The Prophet has a Higher Claim on the Believers than They Have on their Own Selves

After all that was mentioned, it has been verified that the main aforementioned elements are present in prophets and guardians, and that their love and affection towards their nations is the strongest and deepest than the love and affection of anyone else. These emotions are not wild or ambiguous but rather original, sincere and founded upon the feeling of responsibility and the ownership of a thorough, holistic and realistic outlook which is based on personal unique capacities rather than revelation.

Moreover, due to the fact that this outlook is reliant upon divine support and possesses abstention from error, inattentiveness, forgetfulness, injustice and extremism as a fixed and true guarantee, - due to all of the above-, it is natural that the Prophet ﷺ and the Imām ؑ acquire guardianship – in its wider and more precise context – over the people, all the people.

God ﷻ says:

﴾*Your guardian is only God, His Apostle, and the faithful who maintain the prayer and give the zakāt while bowing down.*﴿[22]

In fact, if man – in his guardianship over himself let alone over another – gets dominated by his internal tendencies and subjugated by his lusts, instincts and interests whenever they overwhelm his emotionally-packed mind and limit its effectiveness, or whenever the emotions themselves overpower the intellect, and whereby he is prone to err in many of his assumptions since he does not have the realistic outlook on a lot of things due to their inaccessibility to the immaterial world and revelation, in addition to other issues to which man – this weak and limited being – may be exposed to, then it is natural that the Prophet ﷺ has a higher claim on the believers than they have on their own selves, let alone their parents... All this explains to us His ﷻ saying:

---

[22] Sūrat al-Māʾidah, Verse 55.

﴾*The Prophet is closer to the faithful than their own souls.*﴿[23]

Actually, the guardianship is restricted to God ﷻ, the Prophet ﷺ and the Imām ؑ in the verse:

﴾*Your guardian is only God, His Apostle, and the faithful who maintain the prayer and give the zakāt while bowing down.*﴿[24]

This tells us that the guardianship of those who are mentioned in this noble verse cancels every guardianship countering it; for, it is the only true and realistic guardianship. And everything besides it stems from it and therefore occupies a space inasmuch as it does not oppose or counter the (true) guardianship.

Based on the above, and upon observing the nation's intuition that realized that this government and guardianship is divine (Godly) – for God ﷻ is the origin and to Him ﷻ return all things – and that – through it – He bestows upon them life, dignity and happiness - by

---

[23] Sūrat al-Aḥzāb, Verse 6.

[24] Sūrat al-Mā'idah, Verse 55.

observing all that - their connection and attraction to Him ﷻ through their intellects, hearts, emotions and entire being are fortified and, accordingly, love arises and so does sacrifice for His sake. Several Qur'ānic, prophetic and Imām-based texts – which have no place to be mentioned in this study – emphasize on this love for God, His Messenger and Imāms ﷺ.[25]

---

[25] The author mentioned some of these texts in his essay *al-Ḥobb fi al-Tashrī' al-Islāmi* (Love in Islamic Legislation) and in his book *Dirasāt wa Buhuth fi al-Tārīkh wal-Islam* (Studies and Researches on History and Islam), in the first section of the second volume.

The Guardianship of the Jurist is Inclusive of All Requirements

We still have to point out to the fact that whenever the immaculate Imām is rendered incapable of exercising his entire role in leading, guiding and taking care of the nation, due to the emergence of some forceful obstacles as is the case with our Awaited Imām Muḥammad al-Mahdī al-Ḥujjah ☙ (May God decree us to be amongst his supporters, helpers and the martyrs who are martyred between his hands...), and since it is inevitable that a nation must have a leader and director who governs its movement and oversees its affairs and law enforcement therein, and due to the fact that this mission is given to only one of its nation's members – not more – as it is narrated that Imām Ja'far al-Sādiq ☙ said, "What is it with you and leaderships! Indeed, Muslims have but one head"[26], and Imām ʿAlī ☙ said, "Partnership in ownership leads to turmoil"[27], we find that Islam – in

---

[26] al-Kashshī, Muḥammad b. ʿUmar, *Ikhtīyār Maʿrifat al-Rijāl*, p. 293, *Qisār al-Jumal*, Vol. 1, p. 262, and al-Mīrzā al-Nūrī, *Mustadrak al-Wasāʾil*, Vol. 2, p. 322.

[27] al-Tamīmī, ʿAbd al-Wāḥid, *Ghurar al-Hikam wa Durar al-Kalim* (printed out with the Persian translation) Vol. 1, p. 83.

choosing this individual – is aligned with the primordial nature as well. We find it choosing the most knowledgeable of the divine proposition which he is supposed to implement to the best and most thorough extent and the most informed person in the nation's reality and circumstances who possesses the slightest level of capacity and competence which impacts the mission he is entrusted with. Furthermore, despite the fact that the level of absolute infallibility is absent in the fallible individual, nonetheless, the faculty of justice and piety acts as a natural guarantee which ensures the fact that everything that comes from him is in the righteous path and according to the nation's interests.[28]

Moreover, his increasing sense of religious responsibility does not leave him any room for slacking or recklessness in implementing the mission he is entrusted with.

---

[28] It is noticed that justice does not lie in the person who is given the right to oversee and manage the family's affairs.

For, the aforementioned elements are also present in the guardian jurist to the extent that preserves the security and natural perfection of the nation in the shades of divine upbringing.

Well-known Texts

Some of the aforementioned was pointed out in the following texts:

Imām ʿAlī ﷺ said in one of his speeches, "For, the materializing of the affairs and rulings are carried out on the hands of those who are knowledgeable of God...etc."[29]

He ﷺ also said, "An Imām (leader) needs a rational heart, an eloquent tongue and embedded courage to establish righteousness."[30]

He ﷺ also said, "O God, he who governs blood, women, spoils, rulings, the guidelines for permissible and impermissible acts (halal and haram) and the leadership of Muslims (and believers' affairs) must not be stingy, for, his mission lies in collecting money, nor ignorant, lest he may lead them – through his ignorance – towards misguidance, nor harsh lest he repels them with his cold-heartedness, nor frightened lest he may choose certain people over others, not one who accepts bribery lest he wastes (people's) rights, nor one who suspends the

---

[29] *al-Miʿyār wal-Muwāzana*, p. 176, and: al-Ḥarrānī, Ibn Shuʿba, *Tuḥaf al-ʿUqūl.*

[30] Ibid., Vol. 2, p. 873.

precepts (*Sunnahs*) lest he leads towards debauchery, not licentious lest he disgraces religion."[31]

The Prophet ﷺ said, "Imāmate (leadership) does not fit except a man who has three features: piety which keeps him away from disobeying God, patience through which he controls his anger and good governance over those whom he governs to the extent that he becomes – with them – like a merciful father."[32]

It has been mentioned in the Ṣaḥīḥa of ʿAys b. al-Qāsim that Imām Jaʿfar al-Sādiq ؑ said, "You must be pious towards God, He who is One without a partner, and look out for yourselves,

---

[31] As found in:

a. al-Nuʿmān, al-Qāḍī, *Daʿāʾim al-Islam* Vol. 2, p. 531
b. Majlisī, ʿAllāma Muḥammad Bāqir, *Biḥār al-Anwār*, Vol. 77, p. 297
c. *Tazkirat al-Khawās*, p. 120-121
d. Sharīf Raḍī, Muḥammad b. al-Ḥusayn, *Nahj al-Balāgha* (with commentary by ʿAbdo), Sermon/Letter/Saying 127, Vol. 2, p. 19.

[32] al-Kulaynī, Shaykh Muḥammad b. Yaʿqūb, *Uṣūl al-Kāfī*, Vol. 1, p. 336, the chapter of: *Mā Yajib min Ḥaqq al-Imām ʿala al-Raʿiyya*, and *Ḥaqq al-Raʿiyya ʿala al-Imām*.

for by God, a man may own some sheep over which he is a shepherd, and then God finds another man who is more knowledgeable of the sheep than their own shepherd, so He removes the shepherd and brings the more knowledgeable man to replace him...etc."[33]

Imām ʿAlī ﷺ said, "The most entitled person – to this matter - from amongst the people is the strongest to carry it out and the most knowledgeable in God's orders therein."[34]

There are other narrations related to the knowledge of the status quo (the time) and its people which do not have room to be mentioned here.

We also say: There are plenty of narrations revolving around the fact that the most entitled

---

[33] As found in:

a. Kulaynī, Shaykh Muḥammad b. Yaʿqūb, *al-Kāfī*, Vol. 8, p. 464
b. *al-Wasāʾil*, Vol. 11, p. 25.
c. *Kitāb al-Ijtihād*, section 13.
d. Ṣadūq, Shaykh Muḥammad b. ʿAlī, *ʿIlal al-Sharāyiʿ*.

[34] Sharīf Raḍī, Muḥammad b. al-Ḥusayn, *Nahj al-Balāgha*, Sermon/Letter/Saying 168.

person to this issue (leadership) is the most knowledgeable. He is that man who is at the highest level of knowledge and understanding of God's ﷻ provisions.[35] Even though these narrations seem to be addressing the qualifications of the Imām and vicegerent who will succeed the Prophet ﷺ, nonetheless, due to emerging as a response against the enemies of Ahl al-Bayt ﷺ, it serves as an apparent proof of intellect and primordial nature.

Moreover, it is natural for him to be the most knowledgeable and comprehensive of his time and the most capable, closest and most competent in achieving divine goals in regards to applying the Islamic rulings and executing its teachings at the level of government. Due to the presence of these traits in many people at various levels, it becomes necessary to observe the nation's interests and thereby grant guardianship to him who is the most capable of managing its affairs and preserving its interests.

---

[35] Review: "Wilāyat al-Faqih" in 'Umar b. Ḥanẓala, *Ṣaḥīḥa,* p. 53-54, 71-73 in order to access these ḥādīths and their sources.

In the End of this Study

For all the reasons mentioned above, the guardianship of the jurist, who meets all the conditions that make him the Imām's representative, resembles to a large extent the guardianship of the person he represents, which makes him closer and more entitled than a father in managing his child's affairs. For example, if the guardian jurist rules that a boy must go to *jihād*, and the boy's father prohibits him from doing so, then the father should not have any effect and the guardian jurist's ruling shall be executed instead of the father's ruling.

This is only due to the fact that the guardian is more aware of the nation's circumstances and interests and of the religious rulings which must dominate its behavior from one hand, and because – by establishing this ruling – he does not want to fulfill any personal interest for himself nor was it established as a result of a narrow-sighted, irresponsible and emotional urge which might happen to a lot of fathers in many situations.

Therefore, the government of the guardian jurist is - as that of the Prophet ﷺ and Imām ﵇ – a fatherly government, such that it is forceful and imposed, connected to God ﷻ and leading towards Him ﷻ. His sense of religious responsibility which is laid upon his shoulders, in addition to the fact that his guardianship emerged from divine religious making, confers upon his work greater motive force and strengthens and depends people's connectedness towards him; for, his obedience represents the obedience of the Imām ﵇, then the Prophet ﷺ and then God ﷻ. The same applies to disobeying him.

Moreover, the faculty of justice which he possesses is considered as a true guarantee which qualifies him to preserve and sustain the security of the path and the (divine) message in every stance. It also ensures people's connectedness towards him and their trust in him and his stances, which leaves their hearts pure from any trace of doubt or distrust in the righteousness of the stances he takes or the orders he issues.

Let all this serve as one of the proofs of the fact that Islam is a religion of the primordial nature and truth, and of its realism and pragmatism in dealing with things.

In the End of this Study

God ﷻ has made us successful in walking the path of Islam.

Praise be to God ﷻ, and peace and blessings be upon his servants whom he has chosen, Muḥammad and his immaculate progeny عليهم السلام.

The Sacred Qum

Sayyid Jaʿfar Murtaḍā al-ʿĀmilī